Time To Glow Up, Girl!

**Rediscovering Yourself
When the Carpool and Caregiver Days
are Over and
You are Too Young to be Old**

By Rena Jones

Text copyright © 2025 Rena Jones. All rights reserved. This book or parts thereof may not be reproduced in any form, stored in any retrieval system, or transmitted in any form by any means – electronic, mechanical, photocopy, recording, or otherwise – without prior written permission of the publisher.

ISBN: 978-1-969028-00-7

Loperpublishing@gmail.com

Dedication

To my husband, Steve—
Thank you for giving me the space to do my thing, cheering me on even when you didn't quite know what I was up to. Your steady support means everything.

To my daughters, Caitlin and Rebecca—
You are a constant source of joy and light in my life. Watching you grow into the amazing women you are has inspired me more than you'll ever know.

To my sweet grandchildren, Mary Elise, Marc, and Molly Grace—
Being your Nana is one of the greatest honors of my life. You keep my heart young and my spirit glowing.

To Cyndy B—
Thank you for being a tireless supporter, especially when I needed it most. Your love came without conditions or judgment, and that made all the difference.

To Christina S—Your enthusiasm fueled my enthusiasm.

To Montez—
Thank you for your sharp proofreading eye, and for showing me how to wield a curling iron and sharing your makeup and life with me.

AND to Regina P—You were the spark that lit the fire. Thank you for seeing something in me that I did not see in myself.

With love and gratitude,
Rena

Time To Glow Up, Girl! 2
Dedication 4
Introduction 6
Chapter 1: You're Not Done Yet, There's More 1
Chapter 2: Reclaiming Identity and Worth 6
Chapter 3: Mental Health & Mindfulness 11
Chapter 4: Hair Reimagined 15
Chapter 5: Skin Care & Hormones 21
Chapter 6: Weight & Nutrition 27
Chapter 7: All the Little Things That Make a Big Difference . 35
Chapter 8: The Power of Presentation 45
Chapter 9: Reclaiming Your Voice 59
Chapter 10: Movement, Flexibility & Strength 65
A Letter from Me to You 72
Positive Affirmations 74
Youthful Affirmations 77
Nutrition Affirmations 78
Hydration Affirmations 80
Appearance Affirmations 82
How To Say No 84
Internal Victories 86
Affirmations for a Great Tomorrow 88
Parting Wisdom 89

Introduction

From Forgotten to Fierce

I love being a daughter, wife, mother, and grandmother, but there were days in the thick of it—carpool lines, sick kids, aging parents, dinner that never cooked itself—when I barely recognized the woman in the mirror. She looked like she'd handed out every piece of herself and forgot to keep a little something in reserve.

Oh, how I wish I'd had a magic mirror back then. One that could've whispered, "Sweet girl, your best days aren't behind you—they're ahead waiting for you to claim them." That mirror would have shown me a woman who found her rhythm again, her laughter again…and who finally remembered she's still got so much life left to live—and dreams to fulfill.

If you're holding this book, you might be a woman whose children are grown. You've spent decades pouring your time, energy, and love into everyone around you - your family, your job, your home. While you were busy with the tasks and joys of life… somewhere along the way, **you disappeared.**

That was me.

By the time I hit 50, I was flat-out exhausted. Carrying my purse and work bag felt like dragging around a sack of bricks. I was overweight, drained, and couldn't even remember the last time I felt like *me*. My daily uniform was old, saggy jeans, an oversized T-shirt, and scuffed-up tennis shoes.

My closet? A time capsule of faded forgotten fashion - nothing fit right, nothing sparked joy, and everything had seen better days.

The only self-care I managed was getting my roots touched up... and even then, I always waited much too long.

As a nurse, I lived in scrubs with my hair in a messy bun and barely a lick of makeup. And for church, weddings, or funerals, I'd reach for one of those frumpy, ill-fitting dresses that had clearly expired in the style department.

My life wasn't always like this. Before the chaos of marriage and motherhood, I had style. I had sparkle. I had *flair (well sort of anyway)*. So, tell me—how did I let her disappear?

I can still picture it—getting ready for Friday night football games or nights out with my girlfriends used to be half the fun.

My best friend and I would huddle in front of the mirror, taking turns with the curling iron like it was a magic wand, swiping on eyeshadow with all the confidence in the world (*like we knew what we were doing*). We didn't have fancy tools or high-end makeup (*actually, I didn't own any, but Montez did*)— just a few drugstore basics and a whole lot of excitement.

Somewhere along the way, that playful, girly thrill faded. Life got busy, and the joy of "getting ready" slowly slipped into the background.

Time marched along and before I knew it, I lost myself.

I began to avoid photos. I would offer to take the picture or hide in the background. I cringed at any selfie I took.

I hated shopping. I felt like nothing looked good on me. My gaze always went to my eyes when looking in the mirror or focused on the hair, the buttons, the shoes. I didn't really care to look at the rest. I thought, "Well, this is just what happens when you get older."

AND...*what happened to my energy?*

I remember it like it was yesterday—the wind in my hair, the rhythm of my feet pounding the pavement, and the pure *freedom* of running as a teenager.

I lived five miles from school, and since I was on the track team, I ran home every single day like it was no big deal.

In college, I even took jogging for credit—yes, ma'am, I jogged for fun *and* a grade.

But somewhere between graduation, diapers, and juggling real life, that version of me clocked out and left for the day. Suddenly, running felt like a luxury I didn't have *time* or *energy* for anymore. Again, I thought, *"Well, this is just what happens when you get older."*

But I was wrong.

Now, at 60, I feel more beautiful, more confident, and more *me* than I ever have in my entire life. I wear clothes that make me feel pretty and feminine.

I still haven't mastered selfies, but I don't cringe inside now when I see myself in a photo.

And the most magical moment happened when a stranger came up to me just to compliment me and actually said the words "You are so beautiful".

I cannot recall ever my whole life anyone saying that to me. Now it has happened many times. I never take that for granted, it's so special when someone goes out of their way to give you a compliment.

I have always given compliments, but receiving was harder for me and always catches me off-guard. But why? Shouldn't we be allowed to feel beautiful?

Here's the secret: **it didn't take a complete life overhaul to get here.**

It took a handful of small, *intentional* changes that made a *massive* difference in how I looked, how I felt, and how I showed up in the world.

This book isn't about vanity. It's about **VITALITY**. It's about reclaiming your identity as a beautiful, worthy, radiant woman.

Not because you're trying to be who you were at 25, but because you're ready to become the very best version of who you are now.

So, if you've been feeling invisible, lost, frumpy, disconnected from your feminine side—please know **you are not alone. And you are not stuck.**

This is your invitation to glow up—not just on the outside, but from the inside out.

I'll be right here with you, every step of the way, like a big sister or a good friend, sharing exactly what worked for me, and how you can do it too—no matter your weight, age, or starting point.

Please get out your highlighter. Mark the sections and parts you want to come back to. Use this manual! I have added a couple of NOTES pages in the back of the book. Everything may not apply to you, but I guarantee you will find something to change your life. Because if I can do it... *so can you.*

Let's begin.

—Rena

Chapter 1: You're Not Done Yet, There's More

Shifting from "Mom Mode" to "Me Mode"

There's a moment many women experience somewhere between 40 and 50.

The house gets quieter. The kids are grown. The calendar starts to look... empty. And while there's a certain relief in that, there's also something unsettling.
You ask yourself, *"Now what?"*

But for others—women like me—life didn't slow down at all.

At 50, I was still working full-time as a nurse, managing a career that demanded my body, mind, and heart. Spending quality time with my grandchildren took loads of time and energy. My husband, bless him, could be as needy as the kids ever were. My days were still packed, but I felt more invisible, exhausted, and disconnected than ever.

And the little slivers of time I *did* have?
People always tried to fill them up.
Can you help with this? Can you work that extra shift? Can you pick up something on the way home?

I realized I was at risk of never making time for *me*. That's when I knew something had to change.

It started with one simple truth: **I wanted more.**

The Problem with "Mom Mode"

"Mom mode" isn't just about raising children. It's a mindset we slip into when we spend years—sometimes decades—taking care of everyone else and putting ourselves last.

You get used to running the show, checking the lists, solving the problems. You're efficient. You're dependable. You're always "on."

And somewhere along the way... you disappear.

You don't shop for yourself anymore unless it's practical. You go to your closet, and somehow, it's filled with clothes that scream *function* instead of *feminine.*

Elastic waistbands. Boxy tops. Uninspired neutrals. It's not that we chose "old lady clothes"—they just... quietly took over when we weren't paying attention.

And the makeup? If you even wear it anymore, it probably hasn't changed in years. Same lipstick. Same eyeliner. Same routine you did back when your kids were in high school—because there wasn't time, energy, or space to rethink it. Or maybe you've just avoided it altogether, convinced it doesn't make a difference anymore.

But the truth? It *does* make a difference—when it's done for **you**, not for anyone else.

The hardest part of being in "mom mode" for so long isn't the wardrobe or the makeup, though. It's waking up one day and realizing,

Time To Glow Up, Girl!

I don't even *know* what I want anymore.

I didn't know what kind of clothes made me feel beautiful.
I didn't know what style or colors made me feel like me.
I didn't know what I enjoyed doing, eating, watching, reading—because I hadn't asked myself in so long.

The most heartbreaking realization I had was this:
I didn't know where to begin.
And honestly? I wasn't even sure it was *possible* to pick up the pieces and rediscover myself again.

But I want you to hear this:
You *can* begin again.
You *can* explore who you are now—and love what you find.
You *can* ditch the clothes that make you feel invisible and embrace a style that makes you feel stunning.
You *can* toss the makeup that no longer flatters and learn what enhances the beautiful, wise, radiant face you've earned over time.

You are not stuck. You are simply *paused*.
And this book is here to help you press **play**.

The Power of "Me Mode"

Shifting into "me mode" doesn't mean abandoning your responsibilities. It means recognizing that **you matter too.**

It's not selfish. It's *necessary*.

You can still love and support your family, still show up at work, and still handle what life throws at you—but with boundaries, intention, and a mindset that your glow-up matters.

You're allowed to be radiant. You're allowed to take time. You're allowed to set limits. And you're allowed to say, "I need this time for me."

Signs You're Ready to Shift

Whether your life feels too empty or too full, you might be ready to move from "mom mode" to "me mode" if...

- You feel invisible or disconnected from yourself
- You avoid mirrors or photos
- You're emotionally or physically exhausted
- You feel out of touch with your body, beauty, or femininity
- You want to make a change, but don't know where to start

You are not alone. You are not broken. You are not too late.
You are simply overdue for some well-deserved attention.

A Gentle First Step: Permission

Before we get into the fun stuff—beauty, fashion, wellness—you have to do one brave, beautiful thing:

Give yourself permission.

Permission to say no.
Permission to set boundaries.

Permission to want more.
Permission to glow again.

The Glow-Up Begins Now

In the pages that follow, I'll share exactly how I went from exhausted and overweight to confident, feminine, and energized at 60. Not because I had hours of free time—but because I made space where there was none. I stopped apologizing for taking care of myself. And it changed everything.

So whether you're drowning in demands or facing an empty nest, hear me now:

You're not too old. You're not too tired. And you are certainly not done.

You're just getting started.

Let's keep going.

Chapter 2: Reclaiming Identity and Worth

You Are More Than a Caregiver

For years, your life has been a beautiful mosaic of care: caring for children, spouses, aging parents, friends, maybe even pets. Your heart and hands have been busy, loving, giving. And yet, in giving so much, many women feel like they've lost sight of *who they are beneath it all.*

I want you to know this right now:

You are not just a caretaker. You are a whole, vibrant woman with desires, dreams, and worth that is just as important as anyone else's.

The Invisible Burden

Caregiving is noble, but it's also exhausting and sometimes invisible. When you pour your energy into others, it's easy to forget that your identity isn't only "mom," "wife," or "nurse." You are not just the one who cleans, cooks, listens, or solves problems.

You are a person with your own dreams, feelings, desires and needs.

Many of us carry an invisible burden — the feeling that if we stop, even for a moment, everything might fall apart. But here's a truth that took me a long time to learn:
Taking care of yourself makes you better at taking care of others.

Rediscovering Your Worth

Reclaiming your worth is a journey. It's about learning to value yourself as much as you value your family. It means recognizing that your happiness and health matter.

Think of your identity like a beautiful garden. For years, you've been tending to the flowers and plants of others, but your own plot might have been left untended and overgrown.

It's time to weed out the doubts and fears that tell you you're "too old" or "not important enough." It's time to plant new seeds of self-love, confidence, and joy.

Who Are You Beyond the Roles?

Ask yourself:

- What do I love to do—just for me?

- What dreams have I put on hold?

- When did I last do something that made my heart happy?

- What parts of me have I been hiding or neglecting?

You might feel unsure or even scared to answer these questions—and that's okay. You're stepping into new territory. But the more you explore, the more you'll remember who you really are.

You're Not Starting Over, You're Starting From Here

This is not about going back to who you were at 25. It's about embracing who you are *now*, with all your wisdom, experience, and beauty.

You're starting a new chapter—not from scratch—but from a place of strength and possibility.

There's a beauty that happens as we get older in that we don't care as much about what others think of us. Let's use that to our advantage.

A Turning Point: Setting Boundaries and Taking Back Myself

When I turned 50, something inside me shifted. I knew I needed change—not just for my body, but for my soul.

One day, I gently but firmly sat down with my husband and told him: *Things are about to change.*

For 30 years, I had done the cooking, the cleaning, and a great deal of the child-rearing. I had been the family's organizer, chef, and caretaker. But now? That was over.

I explained to him that I was stepping back from taking the lead in those areas. I would clean up after myself, and he should expect to do the same. My diet was going to change—I was moving to a low-carb way of eating for my health. I asked him to keep grilling, which he enjoys, while I would add salads, vegetables, and healthy treats. He can still eat his favorite foods too, but I wouldn't be eating them, or if I did, it would be a healthier version.

I also told him that he would be responsible for his own laundry, and I would handle mine.

I was careful to say that things between us were good—I loved him—but I needed to make these changes for *my* physical and mental health.

He agreed.

Since then, it hasn't always been perfect. There have been bumps and adjustments. But it has been a lot smoother than I ever dared to hope.

I have also learned that I can eat anything if I watch my portion sizes closely. I still choose to eat as healthily as I can most of the time because I FEEL BETTER *when I do.*

I also started scheduling days and evenings just for myself or for date nights with my husband when I wouldn't be keeping the grandkids.

Don't get me wrong, they're a huge part of my world and I love them deeply. My family is everything to me, but there were times I felt invisible to them—just someone to "do things" for them. Yes, I knew they loved me, but I didn't love *me*.

That realization was painful, but it was also freeing. It was the beginning of reclaiming my worth.

Reflection Prompt: Setting Your Boundaries

Take a moment to reflect on your current life:

- What are the areas where you've been giving so much to others that you've forgotten to take care of yourself?
- Are there any responsibilities or roles you feel ready to release or share with others?
- How comfortable are you with setting boundaries to protect your time, energy, and well-being?
- What would it look like to say, "This is *my* time" or "I need to take care of me now" in your own life?
- What fears or concerns come up when you think about making these changes?

Write down your honest answers. Remember, this is your safe space to explore what reclaiming your worth might feel like—without judgment or pressure.

Chapter 3: Mental Health & Mindfulness

Clearing the Clutter in Your Head

As we journey through reclaiming ourselves, one of the most important, and often overlooked pieces is mental health. Our minds are busy places, swirling with worries, "shoulds," regrets, and pressures that build up over the years. Clearing that clutter is like cleaning a dusty window so the light can shine through.

The Weight of Mental Clutter

Many women over 50 carry an invisible load of guilt, anxiety, and self-doubt. We worry about the future, the health of loved ones, our own aging bodies, and whether we're "enough." Sometimes we replay past mistakes (that was me!) or feel overwhelmed by all that needs to be done.

This mental noise drains our energy and dims our inner light. When your mind is crowded, it's hard to hear what *you* truly want or need.

Rena Jones

Mindfulness: A Simple Tool for Big Change

Mindfulness is simply the practice of being present—paying gentle, non-judgmental attention to your thoughts, feelings, and body sensations. It doesn't require special skills or lots of time, just a willingness to slow down.

By practicing mindfulness, you can start noticing which thoughts serve you and which ones hold you back. You learn to be kinder to yourself, letting go of harsh self-criticism and embracing self-compassion. For me, this included reminding myself that I was made by an awesome Creator that wanted good things for me. This is not a religious book.

You do you. I just want to be open and honest about sharing my journey with you.

Daily Practices to Clear Your Mind

Here are some easy ways to begin:

- **Morning Breathing:** Start your day with 3 deep breaths. Inhale calm, exhale tension.

- **Gratitude Journal:** Write 3 things you're grateful for every day—even small things count! (I didn't write mine but instead stated them aloud.)

- **Body Scan:** Take 5 minutes to mentally scan your body from head to toe, noticing areas of tension and releasing them. I found I held a lot of tension in my jaw. Facial massage helped.

Time To Glow Up, Girl!

- **Mindful Moments:** Pause several times a day to focus fully on what you're doing—washing dishes, walking, sipping tea—without distractions.

- **Evening Reflection:** Before bed, note one positive thing that happened that day or something you did well.

- **As much as you can, let the past be the past.** Focus on now.

Getting Help When You Need It

Sometimes mental clutter includes depression or anxiety that can feel heavy or overwhelming. If you find yourself struggling, remember seeking professional help is a sign of strength, not weakness. You deserve support on your glow-up journey.

Finding Joy and Healing in Music and Affirmations

Part of clearing my mental clutter was remembering the simple things I used to love—like music. I started playing all kinds of songs, letting the melodies fill my home and my heart.

Music is healing.

I danced in my living room. I sang out loud, especially driving to work—even if I was off-key. I used to be too embarrassed to do that. I was so much happier when I got over that feeling. You can too. Those moments weren't about perfection; they were about *feeling alive again.*

At the same time, I began speaking affirmations over my life. At first, it felt strange—almost impossible—because I didn't truly believe the words. But I kept going:

- *I am beautiful and slim.*
- *I am intelligent and interesting.*
- *I love getting out and being around people because I know they enjoy my company.*
- *I am in my glow-up years.*
- *I feel as though I am aging backwards and reclaiming my vigor and youth.*
- *I am happy, healthy and whole*
- *I can live out my dreams*
- *I am brave enough to live my life how I want to live it*

One day, after saying these affirmations, I looked up tickets for my favorite musical artists and bought them before I could talk myself out of it. And then, I realized—I needed a new outfit to wear to the concert.

One step led to another... and another.

That's how small actions build momentum, helping you feel more joyful, confident, and connected to who you truly are. Use these affirmations or create your own.

I have to say, the concerts are so much fun! I go to music festivals, symphonies, plays and enjoy them all so much. As I looked for opportunities, the more they presented themselves.

Chapter 4: Hair Reimagined

Reclaiming Your Crown with Cut, Color & Care

Hair. It's more than just strands on your head—it's a statement, a mood, a memory. It's how we show up in the world. And after so much has changed, your hair is one of the most powerful ways to reflect the vibrant, evolving woman you've become.

During those hectic years, hair often came second to carpools, careers, and caregiving. Now? It's time for a little hair romance. Whether your strands are silvering, thinning, or just feeling a little blah, this chapter is your permission slip to reinvent and reclaim your crown—your way.

Out with the Old: Why It's Time to Let Go of That Same Ole Same Haircut

Still rocking the same haircut from your high school reunion two decades ago? You're not alone. Many of us hold onto a "safe" style because it's familiar—or because, somewhere along the way, we started thinking we no longer deserved to shine (or were just too tired and busy to shine). But here's the truth: you deserve to feel beautiful *today*. Not someday. Right now.

Hair isn't just about looking good. It's about *feeling* like yourself again—or maybe even discovering a version of you that's been hiding in plain sight.

Your Signature Look: What's Calling Your Name Now?

Ready for a reset? Let's ask the fun questions:

- What haircut once made you feel unstoppable?
- What color makes your eyes pop?
- Do you want a low-maintenance routine, or are you ready to play with bold styles?
- Would a shorter cut feel liberating? Would soft layers bring back that bounce?
- Would you love to have hair long?

It's your canvas, darling. Paint it however you like.

To Gray or Not to Gray? That's YOUR Business

Some women are proudly silver and stunning. Others love color—and guess what? Both are fabulous.

Going gray? Use glosses and shine-enhancing treatments to keep it looking silky and luminous. Healthy silver hair can stop traffic.

Time To Glow Up, Girl!

Still coloring? Choose gentle, nourishing formulas. Soft highlights, rich tones, or even a flirty new hue—whatever makes you smile when you pass a mirror.

Extensions, toppers, wigs, braids? Yes, yes, and yes. My granddaughter loves braiding little charms into my hair, and I adore every second. Be bold. Be playful. The beauty aisle is your playground.

Hair Care: Because Gorgeous Hair Starts at the Root

Here's how to love on your locks like they deserve:

- Use sulfate-free shampoo to avoid dryness.
- Treat yourself to weekly masks or deep conditioners.
- Ditch the heat—or use a protectant if you must.
- Massage your scalp to boost circulation (and your mood).
- Take biotin or collagen supplements for hair, skin, and nail health.
- And if you're rocking white hair like me, skip the hot tools—heat can singe and yellow those snowy strands.

Styling Simplified: Less Fuss, More Fabulous

You don't need a blowout to feel put-together. Embrace styles that flatter your face and fit your life:

- A chic bob with a hint of movement
- Loose curls that bounce with personality (try heatless curls)
- A pixie cut that says "I've still got it" (because you do)

Let your natural texture lead the way. Add a scarf, a barrette, a braid—whatever brings that little sparkle of joy.

Your Stylist = Your Secret Weapon

Don't settle for a stylist who doesn't see your vision. Bring photos. Be honest about your upkeep energy. Ask what would suit your face shape, lifestyle, and goals. This is a partnership—and a good stylist can be your fairy godmother with scissors.

My Hair Story: Letting the White Shine Through

I stopped coloring my hair the day I got curious—curious about the glimmering white that was peeking through like a glowing halo. I let my curls go wild, stopped fighting the Mississippi humidity, and discovered a love for the curls I didn't even know I had. I didn't know my hair could be THIS curly.

I remember watching my grandmother brush out her long white hair before bed. I'd hover close by, mesmerized, and distinctly remember praying, "Lord, let me have hair like Granny's one day." He heard me—and blessed me with curls as white and lustrous as a strand of pearls. And I'm so grateful, especially, that I recall that prayer and memory until this day.

Time To Glow Up, Girl!

Now, this might not be *your* story—and that's the beauty of it. Your hair journey is yours to write. Whether you dye it pink, keep it silver, cut it short, or grow it long—it should make *you* feel alive.

So don't shrink back. Don't worry what the neighbors think. Be as beautiful as you want to be. Be as bold as you *used* to be—or bolder.

Because your glow-up includes your crown. And Queen, it's time to shine.

When I first started letting my long red hair go gray, some people said I was crazy. I won't lie, the grow-out phase was a challenge. I truly understood what the old saying means: *it's always darkest before the dawn.* But I was determined to see the end result. For me, it was more than worth it.

My hair is the first thing anyone notices about me. I never could have imagined that having white hair could be so much fun and so freeing. No more coloring or being self-conscious about my "roots" showing.

I personally tried all kinds of hair gels, mousses, and conditioners before discovering the perfect shampoo and conditioner that kept my white hair bright and healthy.

It was surprising to find that a famous anti-dandruff shampoo with zinc worked best—while the trendy purple shampoos actually darkened my hair. I also found a curl-defining cream that finally made my natural curls stay more structured and less frizzy.

Rena Jones

Styling: Confidence in Simplicity (and Boldness!)

Here's my biggest piece of advice: **Go for it.**

Whatever your hair dreams are—extensions, blonde highlights, growing it long and healthy—do whatever it takes to make them happen.

Research your options, experiment, and don't be afraid to try new things.

And here's a bold move that helped me: find a woman whose hair you admire, be brave enough to ask who her stylist is, and make yourself an appointment. You deserve to have a hair routine—and a stylist—that makes you feel radiant every day.

One important tip: **Don't announce your plans to everyone before you're ready.**

Giving people the chance to tell you why you *shouldn't* do something can slow you down or shake your confidence. Keep your vision close until you feel ready to share your beautiful transformation.

Chapter 5: Skin Care & Hormones

Understanding the Connection Between Hormones, Energy, and Your Glow

As women enter their 50s and beyond, hormonal changes dramatically affect not just how we feel inside but how our skin looks and behaves.

It's easy to blame "age" for dullness, dryness, or sagging skin—but the real culprit often lies deeper: your hormones.

Why Hormones Matter

Hormones like estrogen, progesterone, testosterone, and thyroid hormones play a vital role in keeping your skin hydrated, elastic, and glowing. When these levels drop—whether naturally with menopause or due to surgery like hysterectomy—the skin can become thinner, dryer, and less resilient.
But hormones don't just affect your skin. They also impact your **energy levels, mood, metabolism, and overall sense of well-being**.

Get Your Hormones Checked

One of the best steps you can take in your glow-up journey is to have your hormones and thyroid levels checked by a healthcare provider who *truly understands* women's health—not just by looking at numbers on a chart, but by listening to how you feel.

My Nurse Practitioner specializes in women's health, and I truly believe she saved my life—or at least my quality of life. Thank you, Kimberly Schlagel Bartels!

When I first saw her, I was exhausted, struggling to keep up with my daily routine. After thorough testing, she said:

"It's no wonder you have no energy. You have severe anemia, severely low thyroid hormones, and low testosterone."

Testosterone? I thought that was just for men. But it isn't. Women need it too, especially as it helps maintain muscle mass, bone strength, and yes—energy and libido.

Addressing these imbalances, combined with my hysterectomy, **blasted my energy levels up**. Suddenly, I had the stamina to pursue passions I'd set aside, like becoming an author, and embracing a fuller, richer life.

Skin Care Tips for Hormonal Changes

- **Hydrate deeply:** Hormonal shifts dry out skin, so invest in rich, nourishing moisturizers and hydrating serums.

- **Use gentle exfoliation:** This encourages cell turnover, revealing fresh, glowing skin without irritation.

- **Protect your skin:** Sun damage accelerates aging, so sunscreen is non-negotiable.

- **Consider targeted treatments:** Ingredients like retinol, peptides, and hyaluronic acid can help restore firmness and texture.

- **Listen to your body:** Your skin reflects your overall health, so nourishing yourself inside and out is key.

My Personal Skin Care Routine

Over the years, I've learned that great skin care isn't about complicated rituals but consistent, loving care tailored to *you*—especially as hormones change.

Here's what works for me:

- **Frequent exfoliation:** Keeping dead skin cells at bay helps my skin stay fresh and radiant. I use exfoliators suited for mature skin to avoid irritation.

- **Daily moisturization:** Hydrating my skin morning and night is non-negotiable. It feels like giving my face a soft, protective hug.

- **A miracle cream:** My Nurse Practitioner formulated a cream specifically for me and others facing hormonal shifts. It's packed with vitamin C and estrogen, and honestly, it's magic. This cream has helped restore firmness and glow in ways I hadn't thought possible. Talk to your doctor about topical estrogen!

I also got brave and tried BOTOX® on my "elevens"—those vertical lines between my eyebrows that made me look angry or frustrated in every picture. No more. That unintentional grimace is a thing of the past, and I'm so glad to leave it there.

One more thing I can't recommend enough is **gua sha**. After moisturizing, I massage my face in upward and outward motions with my hands and a gua sha tool (adding additional oils, lotions, or creams to facilitate the gliding motion). Don't forget your neck.

The gentle gliding motion stimulates circulation and eliminates the puffiness. I was truly astounded by how much it improved the look and feel of my face. It's a relaxing, rejuvenating ritual that I look forward to. This is the first thing I did that gave me VISIBLE results within days.

Dermaplaning

Now, let me put you onto one of the best glow-up secrets out there: dermaplaning.

Dermaplaning wands, small razors with a long handle are easy to find and inexpensive. Many women use them to shape brows, but they can be used over the entire face with beautiful results.

Time To Glow Up, Girl!

I know it sounds a little intimidating—but it's *easy*. It is exfoliation's glamorous cousin. A gentle little scrape across the skin, and just like that, all the dull dead skin and peach fuzz are *gone*. What's left? Smooth, fresh, radiant skin that feels like satin and looks lit from within.

And no...it will not cause your facial hair to grow back coarse and beard-like. If it did, the models wouldn't be doing it.

I couldn't believe the difference the first time I did it (*yes you can easily do it yourself*). My foundation stopped clinging to dry patches, my skin care soaked in like a dream, and my face looked polished without a stitch of makeup. It's like giving your face a clean slate.

If you haven't tried it yet, girl, you are missing out. It's one of those little luxuries that makes you feel high maintenance in the *best* way.

What To Do About Sunspots

Sun damage can add up over the years and can leave dark spots that are difficult to fade. There are things you can do. Retinol helps over time.

Niacinamide (also known as vitamin B3) is a powerhouse ingredient in skincare—and it's especially beneficial for mature skin. It helps fade dark spots, discoloration, and dullness, leaving your skin more radiant and even-toned. With regular use, niacinamide can visibly shrink enlarged pores and refine skin texture. Bonus: It plays well with others—niacinamide is gentle and works beautifully alongside ingredients like hyaluronic acid, retinol, peptides, and vitamin C.

Sunscreen prevents further damage.

Chemical peels done by an aesthetician can also dramatically bring back a youthful glow.

There's also BBL (broadband light therapy) which is little zapping laser treatment that is quick with very minimal discomfort.

I won't go too much into this area because the field of skin care is advancing rapidly. In a year any recommendation could be obsolete, but be sure, if you have sun damage, there are things that can dramatically improve your skins appearance.

Chapter 6: Weight & Nutrition

Embracing Your Physical Glow-Up

I was overweight—definitely carrying more than I wanted to.

And yes, part of me *did* want to fit into cuter clothes and feel confident when I caught a glimpse of myself in the mirror. There's nothing wrong with that. Wanting to look good isn't shallow—it's human.

But I was craving something more. I wanted to feel *better* in my body. I wanted energy. I wanted to move without aching, wake up without feeling like I hadn't slept, and feel like my youthful self again—not just the tired, old worn-down version I'd gotten used to.

Getting healthy wasn't about chasing some impossible ideal. It was about showing up for myself. I had told myself I could do this. Now it was time to put words into action.

It was about being grateful for and honoring my body, not just for how it looks, but for all it does for me, every single day.

And you know what? Liking what you see in the mirror? That's a *beautiful* bonus. Feeling great in the dress...priceless.

Starting with Food

My first step was switching to a healthy, low-carb diet focused on minimally processed meats and plenty of vegetables. I avoid foods and drinks containing sugar on a routine basis and save it for special occasions.

I made protein the star of my plate because it helped me feel full and sustained muscle.

I also took collagen supplements, which helped smooth some of the crepiness in my skin—another small but joyful win.

I personally prefer collagen/protein powders rather than ready-to-drink types. I have more control over what goes into them.

I add protein powder to my blender with **frozen** berries, coconut, or almond milk. After blending it's just like drinking a healthy milkshake.

This was a game changer for me. It keeps me full and is a treat. You cannot feel deprived when having a milkshake every day!

I also found a powdered collagen coffee creamer. I feel collagen played a significant part in my glow-up.

But changing my diet wasn't enough.

Facing the Truth About Overeating

I had to admit something hard: *I was overeating.*

Food had become my comfort and my entertainment. I reached for snacks or meals not because I was hungry, but because it filled an emotional space.

A New Approach to Eating

Looking in the mirror while speaking my affirmations every day, I became resolved to embrace my physical glow-up.

I made a conscious choice: **stop eating when I was about 80% full.**

I became more intentional with my portion sizes until I found my sweet spot—the balance where I was nourishing my body while still making steady progress.

I don't count calories—that's just my personal preference. I know it works wonders for some, *but for me*, keeping portions in check and focusing on whole, healthy foods has been enough.

And when I'm at a celebration—like a wedding—and the cake calls my name? I'll answer. I simply enjoy a very thin slice, just enough to savor it.

I'm a fan of the "three-bite rule"—the first bite is the most delicious, the second confirms it, and the third is just for joy. If I feel I wouldn't be satisfied with just a little taste, I kindly skip it. It's about choosing what honors both your body *and* your glow-up goals.

I made a conscious choice to stop chasing that old, overstuffed feeling after every meal. Instead, I began to welcome true hunger signals—the gentle growl, that subtle nudge from my body saying, "Alright, it's time to eat." I learned to eat *out of need*, not out of habit, emotion, or boredom.

And here's the truth: you've got to *embrace* this mindset shift. Don't dread it. Don't treat it like a punishment. See it as a return to alignment—with your body, your instincts, your strength. That change in perspective? It's powerful.

This isn't just what you do—it's who you *are becoming.* Confident. In control. And fully in tune with the incredible woman you're meant to be.

Diet Over Exercise

I also learned I couldn't out-exercise a poor diet.

When I exercised too vigorously, my appetite became ravenous, and I'd often overeat to compensate.

I focused on controlling **_portion_s**.

One simple trick was switching to a "salad plate" instead of a full-size dinner plate, naturally limiting how much I ate without feeling deprived.

After I became used to eating smaller portions, I changed back to my regular plate and just enjoyed the fact that food was no longer dictating my life and that I was in control over what I ate. No longer feeling the need to fill the plate.

Awaiting hunger signals before eating has become something I have learned to flex like a muscle.

I understand there may be medical reasons you may not want to go for too long without eating. **You should always follow medical advice. My medical**

caregiver was involved in my dietary changes all along the way.

I would also like to add that if you need help with weight loss that's above and beyond, there are options to help. Many people see terrific results with GLP1s and other interventions. Talk with your medical/weight loss specialist.

Some ladies also find that utilizing waist trainers and corsets is helpful. There are all kinds of body smoothing garments out there.

Go wild, experiment. Have fun. I can *personally* say it's almost impossible to overeat if you are wearing a snuggly fitting shaper. Something to consider.

Hydration & Energy

I discovered hydration was key. Sometimes I thought I was hungry when I was actually THIRSTY.

Adding a splash of lemon to my water made it much more enjoyable—and surprise, surprise, I actually *wanted* to drink more.

On days when I needed a little extra something, I reached for flavored drink powders—zero calories but full of taste. Some even had added collagen, which felt like a little bonus treat for my skin.

I treated myself to a few tall, slim glass water bottles that felt good in my hand and looked pretty sitting on the counter. And yes, I even found some with cute handles in fun, feminine colors—because hydration should feel just as stylish as it is healthy.

Now I carry my water everywhere I go. Sip, sip, *glow*, honey!

The result? I began to lose weight steadily, but more importantly—I gained energy.

Hydration truly improved my skin! I used to hate drinking water. No more, honey. When I saw the value of hydration I jumped all-in.

Hot/cold teas are their own subject. There is a tea for every occasion. There are even cake and cookie flavored teas.

Some of you waste a WHOLE DAYS' calories on a loaded tea or fancy coffee.

Not me. No way. I make my own. I have my own frothing tool, flavorings and add my own touches. Teas and coffee are a DAILY treat for me. They take the place of snacking for me. I wish that I had discovered this sooner.

Buy the pretty travel mugs and use them. Experiment with teas, espressos and flavored waters. They will enrich your life. Make it a ritual for yourself. Trust me on this one.

No more post-meal naps. No more sluggish afternoons from overeating and snacking. You want to feel light, even after eating.

Even if you are eating healthy foods, **OVEREATING IS OVEREATING.** If you feel your belly stretching, you are overeating. Do not eat if you are not hungry...***sip tea.***

The Sweet Victory of Feeling Good in Your Skin

There's something quietly powerful—almost magical—about slipping into a dress and having it fit *just right*.

No tugging, no adjusting, no deep sighs in the mirror. Just a smooth zip, a glance, and that spark of "Oh, yes ma'am, I still got it."

Now let's be clear: this isn't about chasing some unrealistic ideal or punishing yourself into a smaller size.

This is about *freedom*.

Freedom to move, to dance, to breathe easy in your jeans. It's about treating your body like the beautiful, capable vessel it is—and watching it respond with grace, strength, and style.

When the scale shifts and your energy lifts, so does your spirit. You walk taller. You say "yes" to more things.

Clothes don't just fit better—they express you better. That favorite blouse you once avoided? Now it's front and center, honey.

And the confidence that comes with it? *That's not just fashion, it's fierceness.*

And sure, maybe there's a little sweet satisfaction in surprising a few folks along the way—the ones who counted you out, overlooked you, or thought you were past your prime.

Let them wonder how you're glowing, thriving, and living your best life like it's a full-time job. Because it *is*—and you're nailing it.

Glowing up isn't just a look—it's a lifestyle. And when your outside finally matches the strength and sparkle you've always had on the inside? That, my friend, is the kind of revenge that doesn't need a single word. *Just a wink, a strut, and a smile.*

Chapter 7: All the Little Things That Make a Big Difference

Lashes, Lemon Water, and Learning to Love Myself Again

Sometimes, it's not the big things like weight loss or skincare breakthroughs that make the biggest difference, it's the *little changes* that boost your confidence in surprisingly powerful ways.

For me, one of those little things was... **lashes.**

I've always had "adequate" lashes. A good mascara could bring them to life, but I decided I wanted to try something new—**false lashes.**

Let me tell you, it was a fiasco.
I tried strip lashes. I tried magnetic lashes. I looked like I had a caterpillar walking across my face. No matter what I did, they were never the right fit or shape. I couldn't get the hang of the glue. They drooped, twisted, popped off—I was over it.

Then something caught my eye—my daughter Caitlin's lashes were looking downright stunning. Now, Caitlin's always been a beauty with her long red hair, but like many redheads, her lashes had always been on the lighter, less dramatic side. So I asked her, "Alright now, what's your secret?"

She showed me her secret: **under-the-lash cluster extensions**.

I laughed and told her there was *no way* I could manage those—not after my disaster with strip lashes. But she assured me, these were much easier.

She ordered me a set, along with a bond-and-sealer duo that looked just like a tube of mascara. She gave me a few pieces of simple advice that changed everything:

- Use a magnifying mirror (which I already had—and believe every woman should!)

- Use tweezers to position the lashes holding from the tips

- **Let the glue do all the work.**

That was it. I swiped on the bond, touched the lash clusters to the underside of my lashes... and it worked. **They looked amazing. I felt amazing.**

I was instantly captivated. Ladies, never underestimate the power of well-groomed lashes and brows—they're the elegant frame that elevates your entire look. This isn't a suggestion—it's a glow-up essential. Think of it as a finishing touch that frames the masterpiece.

Now on the days I wear them, I don't even bother with mascara. It's one of those small changes that gave me a huge boost of confidence.

I looked more awake, more feminine, and I *felt* put-together, even on ordinary days. The added benefit...

no more dark smudges under my eyes by the end of the day!

Now, I will say—be kind to your natural lashes. Gentle removal is a must. Use the proper remover and consider treating your lashes with a conditioning serum on your off-days or overnight. I personally love sizes 10 and 12 for a soft, natural flutter. And the best part? They were incredibly affordable—unlike those magnetic lashes I tried (and failed!) to love.

Let's talk brows, honey. They frame the face and can take you from tired to totally lifted in under five minutes—if done right. Now, waxing? I've about had enough of that. It pulls at the delicate skin around the eyes, and frankly, I don't need any help speeding up gravity. Tweezing? Bless it, but it's not as easy as it used to be. My vision isn't as sharp as it once was, but give me a good, high-powered magnifying mirror and I can still do justice. That said, my go-to these days is brow threading. Yes, it stings. It will definitely make you blink twice—but it's over before you can say "hashtag flawless," and the precision is unmatched. Bonus points? Most places will tint your brows too, so you leave feeling polished, defined, and just a little bit fierce.

The Wonders of Self-Tanner

Another little thing that made a *big* difference in how I felt about myself? **Self-tanner.**

As a woman with a very fair complexion, I always admired women of color and women with that golden, healthy-looking glow. There's just something about a bit of color that brings out your features, makes you look more vibrant, and yes—can even help you look a little more toned as you lose weight. Now don't get me wrong. I'm not ashamed of my pale skin. I love what God gave me, **just as all of us should love what our Creator blessed us with.** But sometimes a tan can look great.

For years I felt like it was out of reach. I didn't want to sit in the sun for hours (not that my skin would tan anyway—it would just burn!), and spray tans felt too expensive and high-maintenance.

But then I discovered the world of self-tanners—and let me tell you, they're worth *every* penny.

Sunless Tanners: Because We're Glowing Up, Not Drying Out

Gone are the days when we baked in baby oil and iodine on a blanket with the radio blaring (or in the bed of a pickup truck driving to the Gulf Coast...my bestie and I actually did that).

Now, we know better—and thankfully, we have options that don't involve UV rays or crispy skin.

Enter sunless tanners: our not-so-secret weapon for a, dare I say, **sexy, healthy-looking glow** without the damage.

Types of Sunless Tanners:

There's a whole buffet of bronzing options, so let's break it down like learning the Electric Slide (*we were so cool and groovy back in the day*):

- **Lotions & Creams**: These are your beginner-friendly basics. They build gradually and moisturize at the same time. Great for dry or mature skin because they're usually packed with hydrating ingredients.

- **Mousses**: Fast-drying and great for a deeper, instant color. Perfect if you have somewhere to glow *tonight*, but they can be a little tricky to blend. (Translation: use a mitt, girlfriend.)

- **Sprays & Mists**: Best for those hard-to-reach spots like your back (unless you've got yoga-level flexibility).

- **Tanning Drops**: Mix these with your favorite moisturizer for a custom glow for your face. A few drops = sun kissed. A full dropper = Caribbean vacation. Start small, sister.

Application Tips to Avoid the Oompa Loompa Look:

1. **Exfoliate first** – Dead skin cells are not your friend. Use a gentle scrub or dry brush before applying to avoid patchiness.

2. **Moisturize dry areas** – Knees, elbows, ankles, and hands tend to grab color like it's on sale. A dab of lotion helps prevent dark splotches. **But do not** moisturize all over prior to applying self tanner. ONLY the areas that tend to soak up extra and would become too dark.

3. **Use a tanning mitt** – Your palms will thank you. Nobody wants hands that look like they've been digging in a bag of Cheetos. And I have a thick kabuki brush I use for my hands (avoiding my palms) and feet so that I use the smallest amount of product.

4. **Blend, blend, and then blend some more** – Circles, upward strokes, whatever works—but keep it even.

5. **Give it time to dry** – You do not want to transfer the product onto sheets, clothing, furniture. Give it time to dry. Once you're bronzed, strike a pose and stay breezy—any rubbing before it's dry can turn golden goddess vibes into a spotty giraffe vibes.

6. **Most tanners can take a few hours to fully develop and then you shower off to see the developed color.** I usually apply the magic potion before bedtime and shower in the morning.

Bronzers vs. Tanners – Know the Difference

Bronzers are makeup—they wash off. Great for a quick glam-up (think legs at brunch or décolletage at date night). Self-tanners develop over time and last several days.

You can even layer bronzer *on top* of your tanner (after it has developed and you have showered) if you're feeling extra spicy.

The best part? A subtle tan makes skin look smoother, hides veins, stretch marks, and imperfections, and gives a healthy, radiant glow. It's like a soft-focus filter for your whole body. And let's be honest—nothing makes a sundress or swimsuit pop like a little golden glow.

So, go ahead, glow up! Just don't forget your ankles, hands and neck using a scant amount—and don't tan in a bra, you don't want tan lines.

It takes a little trial and error. Experiment to find the brand and tone that gives you the most natural look for your skin. It takes planning to work it into your routine.

Yes, it takes practice. But honestly? **Anything worth doing takes a little effort.**

A word of warning! Aluminum containing anti-perspirant can leave your underarms GREEN or discolored where the self-tanner is.

You may wish to use non-aluminum deodorant on the tanning days

I made self-tanning a part of my glow-up routine. And the day I looked in the mirror—slimmer, healthier, with soft glowing skin thanks in part to the self-tanner—*I truly felt beautiful for the first time in years.*

So go ahead, gorgeous. Toss the towel on tanning beds and UV regrets. A sunless glow smooths the skin, hides the veins, softens imperfections, and gives you that *main character energy*—no sunburn required.

That golden-brown-toned reflection didn't just change how others saw me. ***It changed how I saw me.***

A Little About Makeup

Let's talk makeup—not the heavy, cakey kind that makes you feel like you're about to shoot an 80's glamour shot, but the kind that makes you look in the mirror and go, *"Well hey there, gorgeous."*

Makeup isn't about hiding who you are—it's about highlighting the best of what you've got.

A swipe of mascara to open up your eyes, a little blush to bring color to your cheeks, and a touch of glow where the light naturally hits—just enough to say, "Yes, I drink water and mind my business."

As we glow up, *less* truly *can* be more. It's about enhancing, not erasing.

A well-blended foundation, a little brow shaping, a nude or berry lip that makes you feel polished—it all adds up to that confident, put-together feeling without looking overdone or like it's more drama than daytime calls for.

The magic? You still look like *you*, just a little more radiant and ready to take on the world.

Tips:

- Skin care above make-up
- Blending is key
- Try softer colors
- Heavy black eyeliners can age you, try softer grays, plums, browns and buff them to a smokier finish rather than a harsh line
- Experiment with creams rather than powders
- Get in front of the mirror and play around with different looks like you did when you first started wearing makeup

BUT if you are feeling the glam bug...find a great makeup artist to show you the tricks to look full glam without aging you or looking like you are going through your manic phase (sorry my nurse-talk seeps in sometimes.) That just means you got a little too...extra.

I am all for dialing up the glam when the occasion calls for it—but when I look back at the photos, I want to see elegance and glamour... *not a color palette that went rogue.*
Pick your star of the show—eyes, lips, or cheeks—but only one gets the spotlight.

A Little About Nails

Nails might seem like a small thing, but they're one of those little details that can make you feel polished—even when the rest of your life feels like the hot mess express.

But let's be real: doing your own nails isn't as easy as it used to be. Perhaps it's time to make a change.

The eyesight? Not what it was. The hand steadiness? Hit or miss. And don't even get me started on trying to paint your dominant hand without looking like you dipped it in strawberry jam.

On the flip side, regular salon visits for gels or acrylics can cost a small fortune—and they come with upkeep, damage, and time you might not want to spare.

The good news? You've got options, girl. First things first—let's talk nail health. Keep those cuticles hydrated, take your vitamins (collagen and biotin are your new besties), and don't be afraid to take a break from harsh products. If you want color and glam without commitment, press-on nails have had a serious glow-up themselves.

Rena Jones

You can get salon vibes at home in under ten minutes.

Prefer natural? Stick to sheer polishes, soft neutrals, or a glossy buffed look that makes your hands look fresh and youthful.

At this stage in life, it's not about doing the *most*—it's about doing what makes you feel your best.

If you are going to spend money and time, go for the pedicure and polish. So chic! Look great in those sandals.

Because let's be honest—nobody wants crusty feet. Dry, flaky heels are not the vibe.

You can't be out here *glowing* from head to toe…and having your heels snag the sheets at night like sandpaper. Nothing says 'put-together' like a pretty pedicure peeking out of your sandals.

Chapter 8: The Power of Presentation

Dressing the New You, One Beautiful Piece at a Time

There comes a moment in every glow-up when you realize: *It's time to dump the frump.*

For me, that moment happened in front of my closet. I stood there staring at rows of shapeless jeans, worn-out scrubs, tired t-shirts, and shoes that had no life left in them. None of it reflected who I was becoming. Who I wanted to be. None of it brought me joy.

So, I started pulling the frumpy outfits out—**one by one**.

Let Go of the Old to Make Room for the New

There's something powerful about letting go of clothes that no longer serve you.

That shapeless tunic? Gone. Those dull-colored pants that made me feel invisible? Out. Those old, cracked sandals and dusty flats? Bye-bye.

I realized I had been dressing in survival mode—choosing comfort, function, and camouflage. But survival is not the same as living.

Color is Your Friend (and Your Energy Booster)

One of my most exciting shifts was **embracing color**.

I used to play it safe—beige, gray, black, navy. But now? Now I reach for **bright, joyful, feminine colors**—corals, pinks, teals, whites, bold reds and bright whites.

Color wakes you up. It lifts your mood. It brings life to your skin and brightness to your eyes.

And here's the thing: *you already know which colors look best on you.* You don't need a stylist. Trust your instincts.

If a color makes you smile and feel a little sparkle inside, *it's yours*.

What Do Colors Say About You

Let's talk about color, because the shades you wear say a *lot* before you even open your mouth.

Color has energy. Mood. Magic. And when you know how to use it, your outfit becomes a whole *vibe*.

Here are 9 powerful colors every *glow*-getter should consider keeping in her closet, plus the message each one sends when you walk into a room:

Time To Glow Up, Girl!

1. Red – The Showstopper
Red is bold, passionate, and unapologetically fierce. It's the color you wear when you're not just entering a room—you're making an *entrance*. Whether it's a little red dress or a pop of lipstick, red says, "Look at me. I've got something to say."
Best for: Date nights, spotlight moments, and days when you're feeling your fire.

2. Black – The Chic Commander
Black is your wardrobe's power move. It's strong, mysterious, and never goes out of style. When you wear black, you don't have to explain yourself—you *own* the room with quiet confidence.
Best for: Boss-level meetings, elegant evenings, or any day you want to feel fierce and untouchable.

3. White – The Queen of Strength and Serenity
White may look soft, but she's strong, clean, and commanding in the classiest way. Wearing white says, "I've got nothing to hide and everything to shine." It's crisp, confident, and oh-so-glowy.
Best for: Brunches, fresh starts, vision board days, or when you want that pure, powerful presence.

4. Pink – The Sugar and the Spice
From ballet pink to flamingo hot, pink is blushin' and crushin'. It's playful, pretty, and full of power. Pink says, "Yes, I'm sweet—but I'm also smart, strong, and not to be underestimated."
Best for: Girls' night, flirty fun, or when you want to turn up the feminine energy *and* the confidence.

5. Blue – The Cool-Headed Beauty
Blue is calm, collected, and quietly powerful. It gives off that "trust me, I've got this" vibe without ever

needing to shout. Whether soft sky or deep navy, blue is intelligent, soothing, and graceful.
Best for: Workdays, peaceful power moves, or anytime you want to lead with quiet strength.

6. Green – The Earth Goddess

Green is balance, growth, and grounded beauty. It says, "I'm in alignment with myself and the world around me." Think fresh starts, abundant energy, and calm magnetism all in one shade.
Best for: Nature outings, money mindset days, or when you want to glow with grounded grace.

7. Yellow – The Sunshine Spirit

Yellow is your happy place. It's vibrant, energetic, and full of optimism. When you wear yellow, people notice—and they *smile*. It's like wearing joy on your sleeve.
Best for: Creative bursts, confidence resets, or when you're radiating that "I woke up fabulous" feeling.

8. Purple – The Regal Mystic

Purple is luxury meets mystery. It's the color of queens, artists, and soulful women who aren't afraid to shine from the inside out. It says, "There's more to me than meets the eye."
Best for: Glam nights, spiritual moments, or anytime your intuition and style want to dance together.

9. Orange – The Bold Optimist

Orange gets noticed—in the *best* way. It's fun, playful, and full of bold energy. When you wear orange, you're telling the world you're not afraid to live, laugh, and light up the room.

Best for: Vacations, first impressions, or when you're ready to make memories and turn heads.

And last but definitely not least, Old Money Aesthetic.

Now we're stepping into *elegant* territory. "Old money" style is all about understated luxury, timeless tailoring, and color palettes that evoke *refinement, class, and confidence* without trying too hard.

Perfect for women 40+ who want to glow up with grace and style. It's a category all its own.

These colors aren't just about making a statement—they're about telling a story. The right color **pairing**? That's where the *magic* happens.

It's where mood meets elegance and your outfit goes from "nice" to *next level.* Here are 9 timeless, grown-up, gorgeous color combinations that evoke class, confidence, and elegance:

1. Ivory & Camel – Effortless Sophistication
There's just something so *chic* about this combo. The soft creaminess of ivory with the warmth of camel looks rich without trying—and it's incredibly flattering on mature skin tones.
Best in: Wool coats, cashmere sweaters, silk blouses, or a pair of elegant wide-leg trousers that float when you walk.

2. Navy & Crisp White – Polished & Powerful
This is that "I have my life together" look. Navy brings depth and authority, while white keeps it clean and fresh. It's timeless, tailored, and totally trust-worthy.

Best in: Blazers with gold buttons (yes, please), classic white button-downs, pencil skirts, or breezy white linen pants for a relaxed but refined vibe.

3. Blush & Soft Gray – Feminine Refinement

Blush is your gentle touch of femininity; soft gray is your graceful grounding. Together? They're pure quiet luxury. This pairing says you're elegant, thoughtful, and walking poetry with a handbag.
Best in: Flowy midi dresses, cozy cardigans, or tailored blazers with a silky scarf tied just right.

4. Olive Green & Cream – Understated Earth Goddess

Olive green brings depth and grounded beauty, while cream keeps it elevated. It's subtle, sophisticated, and seriously versatile.
Best in: Safari-inspired dresses, wide belts, neutral trench coats, or soft suede accents for a luxe yet laid-back look.

5. Charcoal & Taupe – Intellectual Luxury

Muted, moody, and majorly classy. This duo doesn't shout; it *purrs*. Charcoal and taupe say you know quality when you see it—and you don't need to chase trends to prove it.
Best in: Wool trousers, cozy scarves, structured handbags, or anything tweed. Add a silk blouse for that dreamy contrast.

6. Deep Burgundy & Soft Beige – Elegant & Grounded

Burgundy is drama in the most refined way, and beige comes in to mellow it out. Together, they give off a "fireside at the château" kind of vibe—rich, warm, and oh-so-glam.

Best in: Soft turtlenecks, suede boots, pleated skirts, or a structured handbag that means business.

7. Black & Camel – Sharp, Classic, and Expensive

This combo is pure class. Black is your sleek confidence, camel is your old-money elegance. It's the kind of pairing that looks high-end even if you got it on sale.
Best in: Long wrap coats, buttery leather gloves, tailored wool pants, or a vintage bag you inherited—or pretended you did.

8. Soft Blue & Cream – Calm, Cultured, Coastal

This is for the days when you want to channel that fresh, sea breeze energy. Soft blue is tranquil, cream adds lightness—it's Nantucket meets Riviera, and it's divine.
Best in: Cozy cashmere cardigans, light knits, soft blouses, or an elegant wrap that says, "Yes, I vacation well."

9. Forest Green & Chocolate Brown – Rich & Rustic

Imagine crisp leaves, leather boots, and a country manor in the distance. Forest green and chocolate brown are grounding, earthy, and deeply elegant—a match made for cooler weather and warm drinks.
Best in: Tweed blazers, riding boots, structured scarves, or anything that makes you feel like you could star in a period drama.

Bonus Old Money Accessory Tip: Stick with **gold, tortoiseshell, leather, and pearls.** Nothing too sparkly, trendy, or flashy. Let the quality speak for itself. Hair should be sleek and simple as well.

Dress to Flatter Your Body—Not Hide It

Every body is different. And *every* body is beautiful. Listen, the real glow-up magic happens when you dress the body you *have*—not the one you're dreaming of, scrolling past, or trying to squeeze back in time. The trick is not chasing trends made for someone else's shape—it's showing up in clothes that celebrate *you.*

For me, I discovered something surprising—I **love dresses.** After years of wearing nothing but jeans and scrubs, putting on a dress felt revolutionary. Feminine. Freeing. Flattering. It made me feel like a woman again.

Don't be afraid to try new silhouettes. A-line. Wrap. Midi. Flowing or fitted. There's something magical about finding the right fit for your shape—and owning it.

The best thing of all, hosiery is no longer required! No more drooping pantyhose or stockings!

Give Yourself Permission to Be Seen

This is big. Read it again: **It's okay to be beautiful. It's okay to be seen.**

For so long, many of us have shrunk ourselves down. We've made ourselves practical, invisible, neutral. But you're not neutral. You're vibrant. You're radiant. You're worthy of being admired, complimented, and noticed.

If you like sparkles—**wear sparkles**.
If you like pink—**wear pink**.

Time To Glow Up, Girl!

If you like dramatic earrings or a bold lip or a lacy dress—**go for it**.

The Power of Polish

Once I started dressing intentionally, I didn't stop there. I took the time each morning to get ready fully. I changed my purse to match my outfit. I added accessories, necklaces, earrings, maybe a cute scarf. I slipped on better shoes and spritzed a light perfume.

These small changes? They weren't small. They were monumental.

People began stopping me to say I looked beautiful.

Not once. Not twice. Routinely.
That hadn't happened to me in years—or maybe ever. I can't even remember.

And it wasn't just that they saw me. *I saw me.*

I looked in the mirror and said, "There she is. There's the woman I've been missing." Yes, I am 60. I'm not 25 or 30. I'm not competing with anyone else. I just want to be the best me (or on my way).

Styles to Consider:

Midi Romantic: Think flowy fabrics, soft florals, and delicate sleeves that flutter in the breeze—this is the dress you'd wear to a garden brunch or to feel pretty on an ordinary Tuesday. A romantic midi hits mid-calf, offering elegance without fuss.

Classic: Think Audrey Hepburn elegance with a dash of modern sass. Feminine blazers, pencil skirts, slacks, business dresses, sweaters.

Boho: Channel your inner free spirit with a bohemian maxi dress that flows all the way to the ankles. Soft tiers, bell sleeves, and earthy colors like dusty rose, sage, or warm amber make this a style that feels relaxed yet expressive.

Shirt Dress Chic: This modern take on classic tailoring offers the best of both worlds—structured and feminine. Button-down shirt dresses with a tie-waist or belt. Look for styles in chambray, linen, or even soft rayon with rolled sleeves or pockets (yes, we *love* a pocket!). Pair it with ballet flats or espadrilles and wear it anywhere from the farmer's market to a casual workday. Understated, classy, and cool.

Sporty Chic Casual Look

Who says casual can't be cute? This look is all about embracing comfort with confidence. Picture this: a pair of high-waisted, well-fitted shorts in denim, cotton, or even linen. Pair them with a soft, tucked-in tee or a sleeveless blouse knotted at the waist. Top it off with a baseball cap or sun visor, and pull your hair into a playful ponytail or messy bun.

It's the kind of style that says, "I'm relaxed, radiant, and ready for anything," whether that's a walk in the park, cheering at a grandkid's ballgame, or sipping iced coffee with a friend. Add hoop earrings, some cute sneakers or sandals, and maybe even a pop of lip gloss—and you've nailed the effortlessly cool, age-defying casual look.

Sultry Date Night Dress (Red or Black Magic): Every woman over 50 deserves a showstopping, head-turning dress that makes her feel *undeniably stunning*. Here's your sultry date night style:

This is the dress you slip into when you want to feel powerful, beautiful, and desirable.

Whether you choose a bold red that radiates confidence or a sleek black that whispers intrigue, this dress is all about *owning your glow*.

Look for a style that skims your curves—not tight, but tailored—with just the right amount of give. A tasteful slit, off-the-shoulder neckline, or elegant wrap front adds that flirtatious touch without trying too hard.

Pair it with a strappy heel, a little shimmer on the collarbone, and your favorite bold lipstick.

This dress doesn't scream for attention—it commands it. Date night, girls' night, or just a night to remind yourself that you've still got *it*. Because you do.

Imagine people thinking... **"She's proof that confidence is the best outfit... but that red dress doesn't hurt either."**

Remember that beautiful and supportive undergarments add to the elegance. One of my favorite things are my *strapless* bras. I never have to worry about pulling up falling bra straps.

The bras today have great support and leave a perfect silhouette. A good bra is an investment. Be sure to care for it according to the manufacturer's recommendation to extend the life of the garment.

Walk Like You Mean It: The Power of Heels (Yes, Still!)

Let's talk about heels, darling. Yes, even now. Especially *now*.

There's something magical about slipping into a pair of heels that makes you feel like you've still got it—because you *do*. Whether you're 45 or 65, a good heel doesn't just elevate your outfit—it elevates your mood, your posture, and your presence.

Now let's get one thing straight—we are not here for foot pain, blisters, or twisted ankles. No ma'am. We've earned the right to be comfortable *and* fabulous. This isn't about six-inch stilettos unless that's your thing (and if it is, please teach us your ways). A stylish kitten heel, a chunky block heel, or a classy wedge can give you that little lift without sacrificing your sanity.

Walking in heels at this stage of life is about reconnecting with your power, your femininity, and your confidence. The soft *click-clack* across the floor? It's the *click-clack* of confidence echoing off the floor like a round of applause just for showing up.

Time To Glow Up, Girl!

Shoulders back. Core strong. Hips lead. Chin up—not because you're trying to look taller (*I am, but maybe that's just me*), but because you've learned the value of holding your head high. You're not just walking—you're *owning* your space, and doing it with grace, sass, and experience.

Practice if you need to. Laugh when you wobble. But don't let age make you tuck those beautiful shoes away for good. Heels aren't about looking young—they're about feeling *fabulous*.

So, wear them to brunch. Wear them to the grocery store. Wear them to the mailbox if it makes you smile. Because you're not too old, and it's not too late to strut through life with style and a little bit of swing in your step.

After all, darling—confidence never goes out of fashion.

Glow-Up Tip Box: Heels That Feel as Good as They Look

Start Low and Stylish:
A 1.5 to 2-inch heel can give you all the polish without punishing your feet. Kitten heels, wedges, or block heels are chic, stable, and walkable—yes, even on cobblestones.

Cushion is Queen:
Look for heels with padded insoles, arch support, and flexible soles. If your shoes don't come with it, add gel inserts. Your feet will thank you after the first hour.

Know Your Width:
Feet can change with age (thanks, hormones). Don't squeeze into narrow shoes from your 30s. Go for wide-width options if needed—beauty does *not* require bunions.

Break Them In:
Never debut new heels at a big event. Wear them around the house first in 20-minute intervals. Bonus: Vacuuming in heels totally counts as multitasking.

Keep 'Em Fresh:
Rotate your shoes. Don't wear the same pair every day. And keep heel tips replaced—clicking is cute, clunking is not.

Walk With Purpose:
Heels aren't just for strutting—they're for *owning your moment*. Whether you're walking into a business meeting or date night, let your heels whisper: "She's still got it."

The Takeaway

- Don't wait until you lose weight to dress beautifully. Do it now.
- Give yourself permission to shine.
- Experiment with color—you'll be surprised how it transforms you.
- Let go of clothes that drag you down and build a wardrobe that lifts you up.
- You're not too old, too big, too tired, or too anything. You are worthy of being seen and celebrated.
- The change begins in your mind before your body reflects it.

Chapter 9: Reclaiming Your Voice

Confidence in Conversations & Social Spaces

When you've spent decades pouring yourself out for others—raising children, supporting a partner, showing up every day for work, keeping the wheels turning—it's easy to lose touch with your own voice.

Somewhere along the way, your *opinion* turned into advice for others. Your *words* became schedules, grocery lists, and bedtime routines. And your *thoughts* took a back seat to making sure everyone else was okay.

But here's the truth: **You still have something to say.** And the world needs to hear it.

Feeling Invisible? You're Not Alone.

Many women over 50 describe feeling *invisible*—in public, in conversation, in their families.

You might be looked over at a restaurant, talked over in a group, or find that people ask how your kids or grandkids are... but not how *you* are. I've been there.

But something shifted in me during my glow-up. As I gained confidence in my appearance and my health, I also began to reclaim my voice. Not loudly or aggressively—but **clearly and firmly.**

I stopped shrinking.
I stopped apologizing.
I stopped waiting to be invited into conversations.

Speaking Up Starts With Believing You Matter

The first step to using your voice again is this: **believe that your thoughts, stories, and ideas are valuable.** You're not an afterthought—you are a woman with a lifetime of wisdom, humor, and insight.

Speak your mind—even if your voice shakes.
Share your opinions—even if they're different.
Tell your story—even if no one's asked for it yet.

It's Okay to Take Up Space

Let me say this plainly:

It's okay to take up space.
Physically, emotionally, vocally.

You are not "too much."
You are not "selfish."
You are not "bossy."

You deserve to be *seen, heard, and respected.*

Whether that means sharing more in conversations, posting your thoughts online, speaking up in your relationships, or even just ordering your food confidently at a restaurant—**own it.** Those around you will get used to it. If you respect yourself, others will respect you.

Glow-Up Conversations: Practicing Presence

Here are a few little shifts that made a big difference for me:

- I started maintaining eye contact in conversation—*really looking at people when I spoke.*

- I practiced not rushing through my words. I gave myself permission to pause, think, and speak with calm confidence.

- I stopped filling silences out of nervousness. Sometimes, silence is power.

- I asked more questions that *I* actually wanted to know the answers to. No more autopilot small talk.

And you know what? People responded differently.
I wasn't being passed over anymore.
They were listening.
Because I had finally started listening to *myself.*

Walk into a room like confidence called ahead and reserved you the room.

Start by owning your presence before you even take a step. Stand tall—shoulders back, chin slightly lifted—not in arrogance, but in self-assured grace.

My secret, when I'm nervous, walking into a room full of people, most of whom I do not know, *I act as though I'm the hostess.* I walk up to someone and say "hello, how are you this evening?".

I'm not especially good with small talk. But I do love to get to know people. If the conversation begins to lag, I simply say *"so nice to meet you, I hope you enjoy your evening"*. It begins to get easier with time.

I also try to remember that people find you the most interesting *if you find them interesting.*

Gift them your full attention. Do not scan the room looking for someone else to talk to, or fidget.

Be memorable. I've heard it said that what people really remember about you is *how you made them feel.* That's kind of profound.

Say These Affirmations Out Loud:

- *I am interesting.*
- *I have value to offer.*
- *People enjoy hearing what I have to say.*
- *I deserve to take up space in every room I enter.*
- *My voice is not a whisper—it is a presence.*

Your brain will start to believe it. Keep saying it. Out loud to yourself.

Learning to Accept Compliments

Compliments used to make me squirm (I still struggle at times). Someone would say, "You look so pretty today!" and I'd instantly deflect—"Oh, I look tired," or "You're just being sweet." Sound familiar?

These days, I receive compliments like they're pearls—I collect them, appreciate them, and wear them with pride. When someone says, "You look amazing," I smile and say, "Thank you." That's it. No disclaimers, no awkward rambling. Just thank you. Because I *am* working on myself. I *do* care about how I show up. And there's nothing wrong with feeling good when someone notices.

Here's the truth: accepting a compliment doesn't mean you're full of yourself. It means you're full of *gratitude.*

When someone takes the time to say something kind, the most graceful and powerful thing you can do is smile, say "thank you," and let it land. That's it. No disclaimers, no self-deprecating jokes. Just own it.

Because you *are* beautiful and you *did* nail that outfit. And yes, you absolutely deserve to be seen and celebrated.

So, the next time someone compliments you, I want you to receive it like a little gift—because that's what it is.

Smile, stand a little taller, and let those words water your soul. This is part of your glow-up, girl. You've spent too many years shrinking. Now it's time to shine and say, "Thank you—I receive that."

Closing Thought

Your glow-up isn't just about how you look. It's about how you *show up*. And that includes speaking up.

You are not finished.
You are not fading.
You are rising.

So go ahead—**reclaim your voice.** The world is listening.

Your doubters should have read the fine print before underestimating you!

Chapter 10: Movement, Flexibility & Strength

Loving Your Body Through Gentle Fitness

You don't have to run marathons or lift heavy weights to reclaim your body. You don't have to "kill it" at the gym or sweat through bootcamps to feel alive again (but if that's your thing go for it).

But you *do* need to move.
You *do* need to stretch.
And you *do* need to treat your body like the masterpiece it is.

Start With Walking

My glow-up started with something simple and accessible: **walking**.

Walking is healing. It's low-impact. It gets the blood flowing, clears the mind, lifts your mood, and gives your body what it *craves*—movement without punishment.

I didn't walk to lose weight.
I walked to feel **free** again.
To connect with nature.

To breathe.
To **come back to myself.**

Even a 10-minute walk after dinner felt like I was giving my body a gift—and that's exactly what it was.

Flexibility: The Fountain of Youth

You know what's more important than being "thin"? **Being flexible.**

Can you squat down and pick something up with ease?
Can you get up off the floor without using your hands?
Can you twist, bend, and stretch without pain?

That's the real glow-up.

As we age, flexibility becomes essential—not just for health, but for independence, freedom, and confidence.

So, I started stretching. Just a few minutes a day. Sometimes in the morning while the coffee is being brewed and sometimes in the evening with music playing. Gentle neck and shoulder rolls, side stretches, toe touches, back bends, reaching and swaying to the ceiling.

No pressure. Just movement.
Just love.

Time To Glow Up, Girl!

NASA's discovery: Rebounding

NASA (yes, the space agency) needed to discover for their astronauts what was *the most effective exercise* for joints, muscles, circulation...all the things. The effect of no gravity was having a negative effect.

After much experimenting, they concluded that *rebounding had the greatest effect on the body.* Rebounding is another name for trampoline jumping. Studies have found that even mini trampolines/rebounders have significant positive impacts on our overall health. Look into it. I have one myself. I find it is helpful for lymphatic drainage as well.

I took the grandkids to our local indoor trampoline park one day and discovered they offered a monthly membership—so I signed up.

At first, I just bounced alongside my grandbabies, but before long, I was going all by myself. And guess what? Nobody even noticed I didn't have kids with me—nobody cared!

What I did notice, though, was how incredible trampoline jumping is for the body. It's a gentle, low-impact workout that engages every muscle group, improves flexibility, and feels more like play than exercise.

Best part? It costs about the same as a gym membership, but it's way more fun! Let this be your little glow up secret. No one has to know unless you tell them.

Posture: Walk Like a Queen

Stand tall, like you're awaiting someone to announce your entrance.

Posture isn't just about standing up straight—it's about showing up like you own the castle. Chin up, shoulders back, and pretend you're balancing a crown—because honey, slouching doesn't suit royalty.

When I began strengthening my core—just a little at a time—my posture improved. When your posture improves, so does your presence.

Good posture is more than alignment.

It's attitude. It's elegance. It's a statement.

You don't need a crown to be royalty. You just need to *carry yourself like you matter.*

Standing tall says:

I am confident.

I am graceful.

I am proud of who I am becoming.

It whispers elegance before you even speak.

Poor posture adds years to your appearance. Good posture takes years away.

Gentle Fitness, Real Results

Here's what I focused on:

- **Stretching daily** (even just 5 minutes makes a difference)
- **Walking consistently** (short walks add up)
- **Core strength** (Pilates, yoga, or bodyweight movements)
- **Mobility** (hip circles, shoulder rolls, neck stretches and squats) **I also practiced getting up off the floor which is a power move if you are over 40.**
- **Using my small step stool for step ups and downs** (be sure to change which leg you lead with)
- **Graceful movement** (For me this was practicing walking in heels again! Also practicing my sitting posture.)
- **Rebounding** (I do it during commercial breaks and between chores) And by going to the local indoor Trampoline Park.

These practices weren't about punishment. They were about *presence*.

This Isn't About Exercise—It's About Love. This is about loving your body enough to keep it moving.

It's about **respect**, not restriction.
Celebration, not shame.

Every time I moved, I reminded myself:
I am strong.
I am fluid.
I am a graceful—and I'm just getting started.

Epilogue: You're Not Too Late—You're Right On Time

If you're holding this book in your hands, you've already done something so many women never dare to do:

You chose yourself.

You dared to imagine something more.
You started asking: *What if I could feel beautiful again?*
What if I didn't have to fade quietly into the background?
What if I'm not too old... but just getting started?

I'm here to tell you—you are not too late.
You're right on time.

Your glow-up isn't about perfection. It's not about chasing youth. It's about *becoming the woman you were always meant to be.*

Become the woman your 13-year-old self thought only existed in movies! Do it for her. Do it for you.

The woman who shows up for herself.
The woman who speaks clearly and walks confidently.

Time To Glow Up, Girl!

The woman who feels soft and strong, radiant and real.
The woman who isn't afraid to sparkle—and here is your permission.

This journey doesn't end here. It begins again every day—each time you look in the mirror and say, *"I love who I am and I'm proud of who I have become."*

Rena Jones

A Letter from Me to You

Dear Beautiful Friend,

I wrote this book because I've walked where you are. I've stood in front of the mirror not recognizing the woman staring back at me. I've felt invisible in a room full of people. I've carried exhaustion in my bones and a sadness I couldn't name.

And now—at 60—I feel more alive, more feminine, more vibrant than I ever thought possible.

Not because everything is perfect...
But because I finally made peace with loving myself again.

I want this for you, too.

I want you to fall in love with your reflection.
To dance again. To wear the dress. To look forward to every day.
To feel worthy of compliments, connection, and confidence.

You don't have to earn your glow-up.
You just have to *begin*.

I believe in you.
And I'm so proud of you already.

With all my heart,

Rena

Time To Glow Up, Girl!

Psst... Before You Go, Beautiful...

If you laughed, nodded, or felt just a little more fabulous while reading *Time To Glow Up, Girl!*, I'd love you to leave a quick review wherever you picked up this book.

It will help more amazing women like you find it—and hey, your words might be the exact nudge someone else needs to start her own glow-up. Just a few honest lines will do (think of it like texting a girlfriend, "Girl, you *need* this book!").

Thank you for spending this time with me. Now go on—*Time to Glow Up, Girl* and don't forget how powerful you truly are.

Love and lip gloss,

Rena

Rena Jones

Positive Affirmations

I am proud of the woman I am becoming.

I have everything I need to succeed already within me.

I release self-doubt and welcome self-trust.

I am allowed to shine brightly.

I walk into every room like I belong there—because I do.

I choose to love myself without conditions.

It's not too late to dream and grow.

My voice matters, and I speak with courage and clarity.

I trust myself to make wise and powerful decisions.

I display strength, beauty, and grace in every step.

My worth is not up for debate and I decide my worth.

Time To Glow Up, Girl!

Confidence looks good on me, and I wear it well.

I let go of comparison and celebrate my own magic.

Every day I grow bolder, brighter, and more beautiful.

I choose happiness.

Joy is my natural state.

I am allowed to feel good.

I create my own sunshine wherever I go.

I find joy in the little things.

Happiness lives inside me.

I attract positive energy.

I deserve to feel good.

Today is a beautiful gift.

I radiate good vibes.

I let go of what I can't control.

Rena Jones

I am grateful, and that brings me joy.

My smile is my superpower.

I breathe in peace and exhale stress.

I see beauty all around me.

I love to laugh

I have a beautiful smile.

Every moment holds something good.

I feel light, free, and at ease.

Happiness flows through me.

My life is filled with joy and possibility.

Youthful Affirmations

I feel vibrant and alive.

Age is just a number—I'm timeless.

My spirit is forever young.

I glow with energy and joy.

I radiate youthful confidence.

I move with grace.

I feel fresh, fun, and fabulous.

My energy is magnetic.

I laugh often and love deeply.

I keep life playful and light.

I'm aging better every year.

I sparkle with curiosity and wonder.

I dance to my own rhythm—and it feels good.

My joy makes me glow.

I say yes to fun, freedom, and fresh starts.

I feel bold, beautiful, and blessed.

I embrace this season with youth in my heart.

I am proof that I can still be fabulous.

Nutrition Affirmations

I choose foods that fuel my body and mind.

I am in control of what I eat.

I honor my body with nourishing choices.

I reach for what supports my goals, not my cravings.

I eat to thrive, not just to satisfy a moment.

I am stronger than a snack attack.

Every healthy choice brings me closer to my best self.

I eat with purpose, not out of habit.

Time To Glow Up, Girl!

My body thanks me when I eat well.

I've come too far to give in now.

I listen to hunger, not boredom.

One choice at a time, I create healthy habits.

I enjoy food that loves me back.

My cravings don't control me—I'm in charge here.

Healthy feels better than any quick fix tastes.

I pause, breathe, and choose what's best for me.

I nourish my body with care and intention.

I eat to feel energized, light, and strong.

Each healthy bite is a step toward my glow-up.

I treat my body like it belongs to someone I love—because it does.

Rena Jones

Hydration Affirmations

I drink water like it's my job—because glowing skin is serious business.

Hydrated women don't have time for drama... or wrinkles.

Sip happens—I choose water.

I'm basically a houseplant with emotions. Water me.

This glow didn't come from soda, honey.

Water is my beauty serum, energy boost, and mood stabilizer—on tap.

Every sip is self-care in a cup.

I hydrate because I'm high maintenance... in the best way.

My organs are applauding me right now.

A well-watered woman is unstoppable.

Water first. Then coffee. Then world domination.

Time To Glow Up, Girl!

Refill, refresh, repeat.

I drink water like I mean it.

I don't chase people—I chase hydration goals.

I'm too hydrated to be bothered.

Cheers to glowy skin and clear intentions.

My water bottle is basically my sidekick.

This queen sips royal elixir... a.k.a. water.

Hydration station—this body's open for business.

Every gulp is one step closer to fabulous.

Appearance Affirmations

I don't wake up—I show up.

I look good because I *decided* to.

This face? Ready. This vibe? Unstoppable.

Confidence is my best accessory.

I dress for the mood I want—fabulous.

I'm not just getting ready—I'm setting the tone.

Mirror, mirror, prepare to be impressed.

I don't do "just okay." I do *glow*.

I put on mascara and attitude.

I am my own style icon.

Outfit? On point. Energy? Magnetic.

If I'm leaving the house, I'm turning heads.

Time To Glow Up, Girl!

I look good for *me*—everyone else just benefits.

Even my pajamas say "she's got her life together."

Getting ready is my pre-game.

Fresh face, fierce mindset. Let's do this.

This glow isn't accidental—it's intentional.

I rise, I glam, I conquer.

How To Say No

"I love you, but that's a no for me."

"My plate's full—and I don't mean dinner."

"If I say yes to this, I'd be saying no to my sanity."

"Ooh, I'm flattered... but that's not in my schedule right now."

"I'm keeping it low-key and low-commitment at the moment."

"Sounds amazing—for someone else!"

"If I had a clone, I'd send her. But alas..."

"As much as I'd love to, I'm practicing the fine art of 'no' lately."

"That's a kind offer, but I'm going to pass this time with love."

"Tempting, but I promised myself a date with peace and quiet."

"Not this time—but keep me in mind for something less crazy!"

"I'm maxed out on people-ing this week."

"I'd rather not overpromise and underdeliver, so I'll have to say no."

"My social battery says 'nope.'"

"Sounds like fun—but not for me right now."

"Girl, I'm practicing self-preservation. Gotta say no."

"That's a generous ask, but I have to protect my peace."

"I'm trying this new thing called boundaries. I think it's going well!"

"I'd love to... but I won't. And I'm okay with that."

"Hard no—but with a soft heart."

Rena Jones

Internal Victories

I did that.

That was brave of me.

I kept my promise to myself.

I showed up.

I chose peace.

I stayed true to me.

Progress, not perfection.

One step closer.

I didn't quit.

I honored my energy.

That's growth, right there.

I made the stronger choice.

I trusted my gut.

Time To Glow Up, Girl!

I said no—and meant it.

I kept it classy.

I did what scared me.

I chose myself today.

That took courage—and I had it.

I gave myself what I needed.

That was a win, even if no one saw it.

Rena Jones

Affirmations for a Great Tomorrow

Tomorrow's got good things waiting for me.

My future is looking real cute.

I've got chapters left to write—and they're juicy.

I've got dreams—and they've got plans.

Life keeps getting better, and so do I.

I'm just getting warmed up.

I'm excited about what I don't even see coming yet.

Each sunrise brings new possibilities.

I'm ready for more joy, more glow, more me.

Tomorrow's outfit? Happiness and lipstick.

I've still got so much life to live.

I'm walking into my next season with style and purpose.

This journey? Oh, honey—it's about to get *good*.

Parting Wisdom

Protect your peace—it's priceless.

You don't have to attend every argument you're invited to.

Small steps every day lead to big change.

If it costs you your joy, it's too expensive.

Not everyone deserves a front-row seat to your life.

You teach people how to treat you—start with how you treat yourself.

Rest is productive, too.

Say what you mean, but don't say it mean.

Energy doesn't lie—pay attention to how things feel.

You can't pour from an empty cup—fill yours first.

Rena Jones

www.ingramcontent.com/pod-product-compliance
Lightning Source LLC
Chambersburg PA
CBHW060340050426
42449CB00011B/2802